VIJAYSHREE R

Avantika's Train to Truth

The Journey to Your Life's Purpose

AF516927

Copyright © 2025 by Vijayshree R

All rights reserved. No part of this publication may be reproduced, stored or transmitted in any form or by any means, electronic, mechanical, photocopying, recording, scanning, or otherwise without written permission from the publisher. It is illegal to copy this book, post it to a website, or distribute it by any other means without permission.

Vijayshree R asserts the moral right to be identified as the author of this work.

All illustrations in this book were generated with the assistance of AI tools. The character appearing in these images is symbolic and illustrative, not a real person. While the character in the story is named Avantika — inspired by the author's daughter — the visuals are not intended to represent her real appearance, age, or identity.

The images are used purely as creative aids to support the storytelling. The teachings, reflections, and wisdom shared in this book are real and are drawn from the timeless message of the Bhagavad Gita.

Any resemblance to real persons, living or deceased, is purely coincidental.

First edition

ISBN: 978-93-344-0592-7

This book was professionally typeset on Reedsy.
Find out more at reedsy.com

"To every young heart and seeker, I, Vijayshree, offer this book as a gift. May Avantika's journey inspire you to discover your path, find purpose, and grow in courage and compassion. Gratitude to the universal consciousness for guiding me. May this story be a beacon of hope, encouraging readers to live meaningfully."

"The Bhagavad Gita offers a way of life that transcends boundaries, guiding us toward inner peace, wisdom, and compassionate living. Through Avantika's symbolic train journey, every seeker is invited to awaken to their true self, live with purpose and meaning, and realize their highest potential. May this timeless wisdom illuminate your path to self-discovery and fulfillment, helping you become a beacon of love, peace, and harmony in the world."

-Vijayshree Ratanparkhe

Contents

Foreword

For Avantika, on your 13th birthday

A gift of love, truth, and timeless wisdom

Dear Avantika,

Turning 13 is not just about growing older — it's about stepping into your own light.

This book is a story, a reflection, and a gift from my heart to yours. It carries whispers from the Bhagavad Gita, wrapped in a tale that gently mirrors your own journey — your questions, your strengths, your choices.

In every chapter, I've tried to capture the essence of what it means to walk through life with clarity, courage, and compassion. Not as a perfect person, but as someone willing to listen to her soul, even when the world is loud.

Sometimes, we draw parallels to leadership, because true leadership isn't about power — it's about living with purpose. And this, my love, is your Purushartha — your soul's pursuit of meaning, alignment, and peace.

May these words remind you:

- That you are never lost — your inner compass knows the way.
- That your emotions are not weaknesses — they are your messages.
- That your dharma is not a burden — it is your superpower.

With all my love, always beside you,
Mumma (Vijayshree)

Preface

This book was born from a silent prayer.

I wished for a way to guide Avantika — not through lectures or rules, but through a story she could see herself in. A story that honors her spirit, her questions, and her journey as she steps into teenage life.

Using the Bhagavad Gita as my compass, I created a train journey — one filled with choices, emotions, dilemmas, wisdom, and wonder. Each chapter reflects an important theme: self-worth, clarity, duty, purpose, joy, fear, detachment, and inner strength.

Though it's written for her, it holds truths that belong to all of us — especially those seeking a life of depth and meaning.

We sometimes draw parallels to leadership, but not in the worldly sense. Instead, we explore how a young soul can lead her own life from the inside-out — with awareness, balance, and love.

This is not just a birthday gift — it is a soul letter.

A companion for her heart.

A blessing for her path.

A reminder that her journey is sacred.

— *With grace and gratitude,*
Vijayshree (Founder of Shree's Essencia)

One

The Boarding Platform – Purushartha Junction

Avantika stood at the edge of the platform, clutching a worn-out travel bag and a heart full of questions.

She wasn't sure why, but something told her this train was important—*very* important.

Above her, a large blue sign read:

Part 1: Train to Moksha City – via Dharma, Artha, Kama

She looked around. Some passengers were running in a rush, boarding without asking where the train was even going. Others stood still, lost in thought. A soft voice behind her whispered,

"Most people don't even know why they're boarding. But this train… it's for those who seek the real purpose of life."

Avantika turned to see an elderly man in saffron robes, smiling warmly.

* * *

"Purushartha," he said. "The four goals of life—Dharma, Artha, Kama, Moksha. This train follows that path. The question is: **Why are *you* taking this journey?**"

Avantika's eyes widened.

She didn't know the full answer yet, but she felt ready to find it.

* * *

Part 2: Finding Her Seat – Setting the Intention

As the train whistled and started to move, Avantika found a window seat labeled "**Clarity of Purpose**."

A soft booklet was placed on the seat. It read:

- **Dharma** – Live with meaning. Do what is right.
- **Artha** – Seek stability, not just money.
- **Kama** – Cherish joy, but don't lose yourself in it.
- **Moksha** – Freedom beyond all desires. Your final stop.

She underlined the line that said,

"When you know your Dharma, Artha and Kama will come as natural stations on your journey."

A man in a blazer sat next to her, looking tired but content.

"First journey?" he asked.

She nodded.

"Mine too," he smiled. "But I used to think success was just reaching Artha or Kama (Solapur or Wadi)… Until I realized I kept missing the real destination—Moksha."

Avantika scribbled in her journal:

"Don't step off the train for temporary pleasures. Stay the course. Let Dharma be the track."

* * *

Part 3: The First Station – (Solapur) Artha Prosperity Junction

The train pulled into a bright, bustling station—Solapur. People rushed in and out with bags labeled "Salary," "Start-up," "Gold," and "Job Security."

A voice over the speakers announced:

"This is Solapur—Station of Artha. Stay if you wish to collect wealth. But remember: This is not the final stop."

Avantika watched people step out excitedly, chasing resources and financial goals.

She was tempted.

But then she saw a small notice on the wall:

"If you chase Artha without Dharma, you may never return to the train."

She stayed seated, hands gripping the edge of her seat.

"Artha will come," she whispered to herself. "But I must not forget where I'm going."

* * *

Part 4: The Next Stop – (Wadi) Kama Joy Valley

Soon, the train halted again—this time at a lush, colorful place called **Wadi**. Music, food, laughter, relationships—everything felt alive.

Passengers danced their way off the train, enchanted by the pleasures of life. "You've *got* to enjoy while you can," someone shouted from the platform.

Avantika stood at the door for a moment. Her heart was curious. Her feet almost stepped out.

But then, she heard the conductor's voice:

"If you lose yourself here, you may forget where you were going. **Kama is a station—not your home.**"

She sighed, smiled, and returned to her seat.

* * *

Part 5: *Staying the Course – Dharma as the Guide*

As the train moved forward, the outside view changed. It wasn't always scenic. Some stretches were dry, slow, or uphill.

Avantika often asked, *"Why is this so hard? Why hasn't Moksha (Liberation Terminal) come yet?"*

Then one night, an old lady sitting across from her said,

"You're still on the Dharma train. That's what matters. Artha and Kama came and went, and you didn't get lost. That's success, my dear—not reaching fast, but staying true."

Avantika thought: *It's not about how quickly I reach, but whether I stay on the right path.*

She finally understood: **This train is not just taking her somewhere—it's transforming her.**

* * *

Part 6: The Final Destination – Moksha City(Liberation Terminal)

Years later, the train began to slow down. A golden sunrise lit up the skyline of Moksha City.

There were no crowds here. No distractions. Just peace.

Avantika stepped off with nothing but her journal and a heart full of clarity. She had passed through Solapur and Wadi. She had questioned, doubted, and grown.

But she had stayed on the Dharma train.

And now—she had arrived.

A board at the station gate read:

"Welcome, traveler. You have arrived—not because you rushed, but because you remembered where you were going."

Avantika smiled, tears in her eyes. She had lived the Purushartha. And now, she was free.

Closing Thought:

"Life is not about how many stations you pass, but whether you stay on the right train till the final stop."

Two

The Reserved Seat (Swadharma Station)

The train had been moving steadily. Avantika had passed the noise of Solapur (Artha) and the colors of Wadi (Kama), holding tight to her Dharma ticket. But now, the train slowed again — not for a major stop, but something more personal.

A sign outside read:

Station 2: Swadharma – Your Reserved Seat

As the train slowed, a voice gently echoed inside the coach:

"Dear passengers, please find your assigned seat. Your comfort depends on it."

Avantika looked down at her ticket.

Seat: **Coach C4, Window 24 – Swadharma Class**

She blinked. "Wait… this isn't where I'm sitting!"

She had been sitting wherever she found space — following others, copying where they sat. But suddenly she realized… **she'd been traveling in someone else's seat all along.**

The Shift: Finding Her Real Seat

She picked up her bag, walked through the aisles, and reached her seat.

It wasn't fancy.

It wasn't trending.

But it *felt right.*

As she sat down, something shifted inside — peace, alignment, clarity.

A quiet voice whispered in her heart:

"This is your Swadharma — your unique space in the world. Only you can fill it. Only here will you truly feel at home."

Avantika took a deep breath.

"No wonder I was so uncomfortable in that other seat," she smiled. "It wasn't meant for me."

Coach Conversations: Everyone Has Their Role

Across from her sat a girl with a backpack full of paintbrushes. "I'm an artist," she said. "For years, I tried to become an engineer because that's what people expected. But it just… never felt right."

Another man nearby, dressed in a simple uniform, added,

"I fix things. That's what I love. People used to look down on me, but now I realize — I keep this train running."

Avantika looked around. Each coach had people doing different things:

- A Brahmin (Coach A) was guiding others with calm wisdom.
- A Kshatriya (Coach B) was monitoring the tracks and safety.
- A Vaishya (Coach C) was distributing snacks and trade items.
- A Shudra (Coach D) was cleaning the compartments, smiling peacefully.

And suddenly, Avantika saw the big picture:

"This train runs smoothly *because* everyone plays their part."

The Big Realization: You Can't Sit on Someone Else's Ticket

Just then, a frustrated passenger walked by. "I want to sit in First Class! Why do I have to be here?"

The conductor replied kindly,

"You can't sit there without that ticket. It's not about better or worse. It's about what fits you."

Avantika remembered something she had once read from the Gita:

"It's better to follow your own path imperfectly than to live someone else's life perfectly."

She nodded.

"If I try to be someone I'm not, I'll only feel lost."

Evolving Tickets: How Swadharma Changes Over Time

Avantika began journaling:

"Just like train classes change—General, Sleeper, AC—our roles also shift over lifetimes."

- Someone driving the train today (Kshatriya) might teach wisdom tomorrow (Brahmin).
- Someone serving tea now (Shudra) might run the business next time (Vaishya).
- And the true test? Whether they serve with love and honesty.

New Reflection: Life Purpose Is the Journey Itself

That night, as the stars blinked through the train window, Avantika reflected:

"It's not just about where I'm going — it's about **how I'm traveling**. My role, my skills, my joys, my lessons... that's my journey."

She thought of the question the old man had asked back at the first platform:

"Why are you on this train?"

Now, she had an answer:

"To grow. To serve. To be *me*. Fully."

Chapter Closing Thought:

"Your Swadharma is your seat. If you sit where you belong, the journey becomes peaceful. If you keep chasing others' seats, you'll always feel restless."

Three

The Coaches of Nature – Discovering Your True Role

The train gently slowed down again.

Outside the window, a sign glowed softly:

"Station 3: Varna – Find Your Right Coach"

Avantika stretched, stepped off briefly onto the platform, and noticed something curious — this wasn't a stop like Solapur or Wadi. It felt more like… a sorting station.

People were being gently guided into different coaches, not by force — but by feeling. Like something inside them knew where they truly belonged.

Coach Confusion: Where Do I Belong?

Avantika hesitated.

A loudspeaker asked,

"Are you in the Thinker's Coach? The Leader's Coach? The Trader's Coach? The Helper's Coach?"

She whispered,

"Umm... I'm not sure."

A soft, warm voice behind her said,

"You'll know when you sit in the right one. The seat will feel like it remembers you."

Exploring the Coaches: Understanding the Four Varnas

Avantika decided to explore.

1. Brahmana Coach – The Thinkers

This coach smelled like old books and incense. Passengers were quietly reading, meditating, helping others with directions.

One smiled at her and said,

"We study the map and share the knowledge. We're the navigators of the train."

Avantika admired their calm, but something felt... not quite hers.

2. Kshatriya Coach – The Leaders

Here, people stood tall. Some were at the front, scanning the tracks. Others helped settle disputes or led emergency drills.

One nodded at her,

"We make sure the train doesn't get off track. We lead. We protect."

Avantika felt inspired... but a bit overwhelmed.

3. Vaishya Coach – The Providers

This coach was full of lively discussion — people were organizing snacks, managing resources, trading ideas, making things smoother.

One offered her a cup of tea and said,

"We make sure everyone has what they need to complete the journey. We keep the train running comfortably."

Avantika liked the energy — it was warm, busy, and full of action.

4. Shudra Coach – The Helpers

Here, passengers were quietly sweeping, fixing seats, helping elderly travelers find comfort.

One smiled gently and said,

"We don't talk much. We just make sure everyone else has what they need."

Avantika felt deep respect for their silent strength.

Finding Her Coach: Letting Swabhava Lead

Back at the middle of the platform, Avantika sat down, closed her eyes, and asked herself:

"What comes naturally to me? What brings me joy even without rewards? Where do I lose myself — in the best way?"

She remembered how she loved sharing what she learned... how she naturally guided her friends... how she found deep joy in connecting dots others missed.

Her eyes opened slowly.

"I'm a **Brahmana-Kshatriya blend**," she whispered.

"I love teaching. But I also like to *act*, to lead with a heart full of wisdom."

She smiled — finally, **she knew her coach.**

Coach Realignment: Helping Others Find Their Seat

As she took her seat in her chosen coach, she saw a teenager pacing, confused.

"Everyone says I should become a doctor, but I don't enjoy studying at all," he muttered.

Avantika walked over and gently said,

"Then maybe your seat isn't in the thinker's coach. What *do* you enjoy?"

"Fixing things... making machines work."

She smiled. "That's the **Shudra coach** — the implementers. Strong hands, clear focus. No role is less. It's just different."

His eyes lit up. He finally sat down.

Lesson from the Journey: No Seat is Superior — Only Misplaced

As the train moved again, the voice from the speaker returned:

"When a navigator stops navigating, the train gets lost.

When a driver stops driving, the train halts.

When a provider stops providing, the train suffers.

When a helper stops serving, the train breaks down.

Every role matters. Every role is sacred."

Avantika wrote in her journal:

"Don't ask, *Which coach is better?*

Ask instead: *Which coach feels like home?*"

Inner Peace through Role Clarity

As the sun set, Avantika looked out the window. For the first time in a long time, she wasn't just traveling — she was **anchored in her nature**.

"This journey... it's not about being everything to everyone.

It's about being *fully me*."

Closing Thought:

"When you find your natural seat, life feels peaceful.

When you try to force yourself into someone else's role, even a first-class seat feels tight."

Four

The Journey Timetable – The Four Ashramas

As dawn gently broke, golden sunlight filtered through the train window.

Avantika stirred from a light nap. The train's rhythm had changed — softer now, like it was easing into a new mood. Outside, a board appeared:

Station 4: Ashrama – Know Your Journey Timetable

A soft chime rang inside the coach.

"Dear travelers," said the voice, "Where you sit matters — but *when* you sit there matters too. Please check your stage on the journey."

Ashramas: The Timetable of the Soul's Journey

Avantika tilted her head.

"I know my seat... but what phase of the journey am I in?"

She looked up. A **spiritual conductor** appeared — serene eyes, timeless presence.

"Child," he said gently, "every journey has four phases. Just like a day moves from morning to night, your soul travels through four stations: **Brahmacharya, Grihastha, Vanaprastha, and Sannyasa**."

1. Brahmacharya – The Morning Prep

"This is when you board the train," the conductor said.

"Eyes wide. Notebook open. You ask, 'Where are we going? How do I get there?'"

Avantika remembered her early years — learning, questioning, absorbing the values her teachers and elders passed on. The excitement of discovering Dharma.

"Skipping this phase," he warned, "is like boarding the train without knowing the route. You'll be sitting in the wrong coach, confused by every stop."

She nodded.

"That's when the foundation is built. The soul stretches... wakes up."

2. Grihastha – The Midday Hustle

The coach now bustled with people talking, planning, helping, hustling. Children giggled. Luggage shifted. Tea was poured.

"This," the conductor whispered, "is the **main phase** — work, marriage, parenting, contribution. You fulfill duties while staying on the path of Dharma."

Avantika observed: some passengers were **enjoying the ride**, mindful of the track. Others were **clutching their bags**, fearful of what they might lose, forgetting the journey's end.

"When passengers mistake the train ride as the destination," the conductor sighed, "they get stuck. They miss the call to prepare for the final stop."

Avantika made a mental note: *Don't lose yourself in the comfort of the ride.*

3. Vanaprastha – The Evening Silence

In a quieter coach ahead, the crowd thinned. Older passengers shared stories, passed on wisdom, and began packing lightly.

"This is **Vanaprastha**," the conductor said. "You begin moving closer to the door — not out of fear, but readiness. You guide others, but loosen your grip on control."

Avantika watched an elderly couple help a young mother calm her baby — and then slowly step back into silence. They smiled, content.

"This is the beauty of detachment," the conductor said, "not rejection — but graceful release."

Avantika closed her eyes. *Would she be able to let go when the time came?*

4. Sannyasa – The Final Stop

At the very end of the train, an almost empty coach glowed in silence.

A few souls sat in stillness, eyes closed — nothing in their hands, everything surrendered.

"This is **Sannyasa**," the conductor whispered. "Not escape — but transcendence. When you're ready to get off the train, and step into the eternal."

Avantika's heart stirred. *One day, I'll reach there. But not yet. My stop hasn't come.*

Leadership Mirror: Seasons of Leading

As she walked back to her coach, Avantika reflected:
"Leadership, too, changes with each stage."

- In **Brahmacharya**, you learn by observing leaders — soaking in values.
- In **Grihastha**, you lead actively — balancing performance with purpose.
- In **Vanaprastha**, you mentor others — stepping back to uplift.
- In **Sannyasa**, you lead by example — detached, centered, peaceful.

"Each phase asks different things from me. And none of them is forever."

Inner Realization: Don't Get Stuck

Back in her seat, Avantika wrote in her journal:
"Sometimes people get stuck in one coach.
Some stay students forever, afraid to take responsibility.
Some cling to family life, refusing to let go.
Others avoid wisdom-sharing, fearing irrelevance.
But the train doesn't stop. Life keeps moving."

Final Announcement from the Conductor:

"Travelers, remember:
Don't skip stations. Don't overstay either.
Each Ashrama has its purpose.
Honor the stage you're in. And prepare for the next."
Avantika smiled.

"I'm still in Grihastha — holding responsibilities. But I now know what lies ahead. And I'll embrace it when the time comes."

Closing Thought:

"Life is not just about *where* you are on the train —

It's about *when* you are, and *how gracefully* you move through each phase."

Five

The Engine Room – Which Guna Is Driving You?

Avantika stood quietly at the doorway between coaches, watching the train's motion.

For the first time, she wasn't looking *outside* at the landscape.

She was looking *inward* — wondering:

"What's driving this train?

Why do I sometimes move fast, sometimes slow… and sometimes not at all?"

Just then, the **conductor** reappeared — this time with oil-stained gloves and a whistle tucked into his kurta.

"Welcome," he smiled, "to the **engine room of the self**.

Here, three unseen forces—**Sattva, Rajas, and Tamas**—decide the speed, direction, and quality of your entire ride."

The Three Gunas - Your Inner Engine Modes

The conductor pointed to a glowing chart on the wall, humming softly like an old magical machine.

1. Sattva - The Serene Superfast Express

"This is the **Sattva engine**," he said, "gentle yet powerful."

Avantika saw herself sitting by the window, sunlight on her face, journal in hand — reading, reflecting, creating, helping. Time moved gracefully.

"When Sattva is in charge," the conductor said,

"the journey feels **light**. You feel **clear, balanced, purposeful.**

You stop chasing stations. You start enjoying the ride."

Bhagavad Gita 14.6: "Sattva is pure, illuminating, and binds through attachment to happiness and knowledge."

When Avantika was in Sattva:

- She spent time in reflection, meditation, reading wisdom texts.
- Her actions were thoughtful, values-aligned.
- Her energy lifted others — even without trying.

"This is when you're not just on the train — you're guiding others too," she wrote in her diary.

2. Rajas - The Busy Passenger Train

"Now," said the conductor, tapping the next switch,

"this is **Rajas** — always moving, but never still."

Avantika saw another version of herself: multitasking, checking her phone, juggling meetings, planning, fixing, worrying.

"This engine is fast," he explained,

"but it makes too many stops. And every new desire pulls the chain."

Bhagavad Gita 14.7: "Rajas is born of passion. It binds through attachment to activity and desire."

When Avantika was in Rajas:

- She was ambitious — productive, energetic — but restless.
- She overcommitted, seeking validation.
- Her joy depended on results.

"It feels like I'm traveling… but I'm not arriving anywhere," she whispered.

3. Tamas – The Stalled Train at the Station

A heavy silence filled the engine room as the conductor dimmed the lights.

"And this," he said, "is **Tamas** — inertia. The train is at the station. But the traveler… won't move."

Avantika saw herself lying in bed late into the morning, feeling numb, scrolling endlessly, doubting herself.

"Tamas hides purpose under a blanket of confusion," the conductor said softly.

"The train doesn't break. You just forget why you boarded."

📖 *Bhagavad Gita 14.8*: "Tamas arises from ignorance and binds through carelessness, laziness, and delusion."

When Avantika was in Tamas:

- She procrastinated, disconnected from her goals.
- Even simple tasks felt overwhelming.

- She felt like life was passing… without her participation.

"Which Engine Is Running Right Now?"

The conductor turned to Avantika gently.

"Your outer journey reflects your inner engine.

Each day, each decision — are you moving in **Sattva**, **Rajas**, or **Tamas**?"

Can I Change Tracks?

Avantika asked:

"What if I realize I'm in Rajas or Tamas? Am I stuck forever?"

The conductor smiled.

"No dear. That's the beauty of this train.

You can switch tracks **anytime** — but first, you must become aware."

From Tamas to Rajas: Take one small step. Wake up early. Clean your space. Choose movement over stillness.

From Rajas to Sattva: Breathe. Reflect. Prioritize values over vanity. Act with awareness.

And finally…

Transcending All Three – When the Soul Takes Flight

The lights dimmed again. A window opened. And Avantika felt a breeze… from somewhere higher.

"Those who transcend all three," said the conductor, "no longer ride the train. They soar."

She saw herself — not running, not chasing, not stopping — but **surrendering**. Floating above the tracks. Guided by love. By Bhakti.

Bhagavad Gita 14.20: "The soul that rises above the Gunas becomes free from birth, death, and suffering — and attains the Supreme."

Avantika's Reflection:

"I now understand:

- Sattva gives clarity
- Rajas gives movement
- Tamas gives rest (but can trap)

But beyond them all… is **Grace.**

When I align with my Dharma and surrender to the Divine…

I don't need to pull the train.

The train pulls me."

Closing Thought:

"The destination is the same for all.

But the experience? It depends on your engine."

Which train are you on today? And which one are you choosing tomorrow?

Six

Who's Driving the Train? – Mastering Mind & Senses

As the scenery outside shifted from city buzz to quiet fields, Avantika noticed something strange.

Her thoughts were scattered. One moment she was dreaming of future success, the next she was craving coffee, then suddenly lost in past memories.

"Why am I not present?" she whispered.

"Why do I feel like the train is moving... but I'm not the one steering?"

Just then, the familiar conductor appeared — this time holding a

control board diagram in one hand and a whistle in the other.

"You've come to the **Engine Room of Inner Governance**, Avantika," he said.

"It's time to learn who's really driving this train."

Mind, Senses, and Intellect — The Inner Mechanics

The conductor led her to a glass window looking into the control cabin.

"This," he pointed, "is where every life's journey is steered — not from outside events, but from within."

Let's decode it through a **train analogy** (inspired by the Gita's timeless chariot metaphor):

Element - Traditional Analogy - Train Analogy - Role

- **Senses (Indriyas)** → Horses → Engine → Power that pulls you toward experiences
- **Mind (Manas)** → Reins → Train Conductor → Responds to desires, steers attention
- **Intellect (Buddhi)** → Charioteer → Train Control System (Tracks & Signals) → Decision-maker, sets direction
- **True Self (Atman)** → Passenger → You — the Traveler → The observer, not the controller

* * *

1. Senses - The Engine (Powerful but Untrained)

Avantika peered into the engine room — it was roaring.

"This is your **Indriyas** — your five senses," said the conductor.

"They're strong. They're exciting. But if you let them run wild... they'll take you anywhere *except* where you truly want to go."

When Avantika let her senses lead:

- She scrolled endlessly, lost in social media.
- She ate out of boredom, not hunger.
- She followed impulses, then felt empty.

The engine is strong — but it needs a ***track*** *to follow.*

2. Mind – The Conductor (Emotional and Easily Swayed)

The next room was filled with dials, knobs, and constant chatter.

"The **mind** listens to the senses," explained the conductor,

"but it's meant to take orders from the **intellect**. Without discipline, it just follows the loudest voice."

When Avantika let her mind get distracted:

- She started projects but didn't finish them.
- Her mood swung wildly with praise or criticism.
- She felt busy — but not aligned.

The conductor must learn to ignore the engine's noise and listen to the signals from the tracks — the intellect.

3. Intellect – The Tracks & Signals (Guided by Wisdom)

Now came the quietest yet most powerful room — the **signal control**.

Red, yellow, and green lights blinked. Every turn, every speed limit, was encoded here.

"This," said the conductor, reverently, "is your **Buddhi**.

It tells the mind what is right. It reminds you of your purpose. It sees beyond emotion."

When Avantika followed her Buddhi:

- She paused before reacting.
- She asked, *"Is this aligned with my Dharma?"*
- She made fewer decisions — but better ones.

***Bhagavad Gita 3.42*:** "The senses are superior to the body, the mind is superior to the senses, and the intellect is superior to the mind."

4. The True Self – The Silent Passenger

Finally, the conductor placed a hand on her shoulder.

"And you, Avantika... you are not the train.

You are the **passenger** inside — the observer, the experiencer, the soul (Atman)."

She closed her eyes. For the first time, she felt **detached yet aware**.

She wasn't her thoughts.

She wasn't her senses.

She was the **witness** of it all.

Reflection: Who's Driving Today?

"When the engine pulls too hard, and the mind obeys without thinking," said the conductor,

"the train becomes chaotic."

"But when the **intellect sets the direction**, and the **mind listens wisely**,

the **senses follow**... and you, the soul, enjoy a smooth and meaningful ride."

Avantika's Journal Entry

"Today I learned that emotional strength isn't about suppression — it's about regulation.

It's about letting **wisdom** (Buddhi) take the wheel.
And reminding myself that I am not the wheel —
I am the one riding with trust, clarity, and purpose."

Final Takeaway: Reclaiming Inner Leadership

- **Don't let the senses (engine) lead the journey** — they only seek pleasure.
- **Don't let the mind (conductor) follow every impulse** — it gets tired and confused.
- **Let the intellect (tracks) set direction** — guided by Dharma, clarity, and stillness.
- **Be the aware traveler** — enjoying the ride, not trying to control every turn.

Closing Thought:

Right now, who's driving your train?
Are your senses pulling you off-course?
Or is your intellect quietly guiding you home?

Seven

Karma Yoga – Duty Without Baggage

The train hummed steadily now.

Avantika, sitting by the window with her journal open, watched the changing scenery with a peaceful gaze. But her mind had questions again…

"I've been doing so much… showing up, trying hard… but why do I still feel this tight knot inside me?

What am I really working *for*?"

As if on cue, the conductor appeared once again, this time with a cup of chai and a clipboard labeled:

"Karma Yoga: Work Without Worry."

What Is Karma Yoga? — Right Action, Right Attitude

The conductor sat beside her.

"Avantika," he smiled, "the train runs best when every crew member performs their duty *without attachment.*

It's not about applause. Not even about the destination.

It's about sincere action — aligned with purpose, not pressure."

What Are You Doing on the Train?

The conductor asked:

"During this journey of life — are you the tea vendor? The coach attendant? The track mechanic? Or a passenger fretting over delays?"

The lesson?

Just do your dharma — with love, without worrying who's watching.

Two Pillars of Karma Yoga

1. Right Action = Choosing the Right Track

"Just as a train must stay on the proper route," said the conductor, "your actions must align with **Dharma** — your higher purpose."

He showed her three types of karmas — just like train types:

Karma Type → Train Type → Description

- Uttama Karma → Express Train → Selfless, sacred actions (Yajnas) — lead straight to spiritual progress
- Madhyama Karma → Local Train → Duty done with personal goals — moves forward, but slower
- Adhama Karma → Derailing Train → Selfish, harmful actions —

take you off-track

The Five Sacred Yajnas (Express Coaches):

1. **Deva Yajna** – Gratitude to Divine
2. **Pitru Yajna** – Honoring ancestors
3. **Brahma Yajna** – Learning and teaching wisdom
4. **Manushya Yajna** – Serving humanity
5. **Bhūta Yajna** – Caring for all living beings

"These are the *fast-track lanes* of Karma Yoga," he said.

2. Right Attitude = Your Mindset While Working

The conductor leaned in:
"Two passengers can be on the same train:
one is restless about reaching, the other enjoys every moment.
The difference? **Attachment vs. Surrender.**"

Bhagavad *Gita* 2.50: "Yoga is the art of work — to act without getting bound by the results."

Leadership Insight: It's not just **what** you do, but **how** you do it.

Goal. Result. Expectation — Three Different Stations

The conductor pulled out three signs:
Concept → Train Analogy → Life Example

- Goal → Where you intend to go → "I want to be a teacher."
- Result → Where you actually arrive → "I became a writer who teaches through books."
- Expectation → Demanding that journey go exactly as planned → "It must happen this way, by this time."

"Let go of expectations.

Set your goals, act sincerely, and trust the train to take you where you're meant to be."

Mini Summary Chart

Role → Train Analogy → Leadership Insight

- Driver → Focused on route → Lead with purpose, not ego
- Server → Serves silently → Contribute without praise
- Ticket Checker → Upholds rules → Stay accountable to Dharma
- Passenger → Present in journey → Trust the process, surrender outcomes

Burnout Analogy – Overheating the Engine

Avantika asked,

"But what if I feel tired? Burned out from constantly giving?"

The conductor nodded.

"Burnout comes from **over-identifying** with results.

Like an engine overheating because it's trying to pull *every coach alone.*

Stay in your Dharma zone. Don't try to serve all compartments — just the ones assigned to you."

Nishkama Karma – Working Without Wanting

"Imagine," the conductor whispered, "if the chai vendor refused to serve because no one praised him...

or if the ticket checker quit because passengers didn't thank her."

Karma Yoga is **selfless execution**.

Do it **as an offering** — not for applause, not for payoff.

Avantika's Journal Entry

"Today I realized — I am not the manager of outcomes.

I am just a sincere part of this sacred crew.

My job is to serve with heart, stay aligned, and let Krishna handle the tracks."

Gita's Wisdom to Remember

"You have a right to perform your duties,
but not to the fruits of your actions." — *Gita 2.47*

"The wise stay balanced in success and failure." — *Gita 2.48*

Final Reflection:

Are you acting like a Karma Yogi — doing your part and letting go?

Or are you still checking the arrival board every 5 minutes, doubting the route?

Trust the train.

Stay sincere in your karma.

The Conductor knows the way.

Eight

Jnana Yoga – Knowing the Route Map

The rhythmic hum of the train had become familiar now. The crowds, the chai calls, the sceneries flashing past…

Yet something stirred within Avantika.

"Am I just going with the flow of the train… or do I *really* know where I'm going?"

As she pondered, a kind elderly traveler beside her handed over an old map — golden, frayed, and glowing softly.

"Don't mistake the train ride for your final destination, child,"

he said.

"This map doesn't show places — it shows *truths*."

What Is Jnana Yoga? — Wisdom Is Knowing the Real Journey

Jnana Yoga is the journey of **truth-seeking** — not through outer conquests, but inner inquiry.

"Am I just this body? Am I the roles I play?

Or am I something deeper, timeless, eternal?"

This is the yoga of the mind that questions, reflects, and *awakens*.

The Train Analogy - Jnana Yoga: Journey from Confusion to Clarity

Concept → Spiritual Insight → Train Analogy

- Ignorance (Avidya) → Mistaking body/mind for self → Passenger lost in distractions
- Inquiry (Vichara) → "Who am I?" → Checking the route & destination
- Wisdom (Jnana) → Realizing eternal Self → Traveling with full clarity
- Liberation (Moksha) → Freedom from illusion → Getting off at the right station, free and fulfilled

1. Ignorance = Lost on the Train

Many board the train of life distracted — enchanted by the window views (material pleasures), gossiping with co-passengers (external validation), or endlessly scrolling their phones (mindless living).

"Where are you headed?" someone asks.

And they reply, "I don't know... just following where everyone else is going."

This is Avidya — spiritual forgetfulness.

2. Inquiry = Checking the Route

Avantika looked at the map, then out the window, then back inside her heart.

"Who am I beyond my job, my family role, my name?"

This is **Vichara** — the first spark of wisdom.

She began asking:

- Is this work aligned with my soul?
- Is this goal fleeting or fulfilling?
- Am I reacting from ego or choosing from truth?

Just like a smart traveler checks train schedules and stations, a Jnana Yogi questions beliefs, seeks knowledge, and re-evaluates the journey.

3. Wisdom = Recognizing the Right Path

Once the route became clear, Avantika noticed something:

She no longer panicked at delays.

She didn't envy first-class travelers.

She stopped getting off at every tempting station.

"This train is a tool," she realized,

"but *I* am the traveler — not the train."

This is Jnana — clarity, spiritual intelligence, and value-driven choices.

4. Liberation = Arriving with Awareness

As the train neared a mountain curve, the elderly traveler smiled again:

"When the body grows old, the train slows down.

But the awakened soul steps off joyfully — because they *know* they've reached their true home."

Moksha is not an escape — it's an arrival into truth.

Not *after death*, but even while alive — through realization.

Avantika's Journal Entry

"Today I asked the right question — not *what* I should do, but *who* I truly am.

And the answers aren't always loud. Sometimes, wisdom whispers in stillness.

The train is still moving, but I now ride it with my eyes open."

Jnana Yoga for Leaders: Making Wise, Soul-Aligned Decisions

Gita Insight → Leadership Reflection

- Avidya (ignorance) → Hustling blindly without clear values
- Vichara (inquiry) → Stepping back for reflection & discernment
- Jnana (wisdom) → Choosing long-term good over short-term gain

Moksha (liberation) → Leading from soul, not ego

Gita Insight → Leadership Reflection

- Avidya (ignorance) → Hustling blindly without clear values
- Vichara (inquiry) → Stepping back for reflection & discernment
- Jnana (wisdom) → Choosing long-term good over short-term gain
- Moksha (liberation) → Leading from soul, not ego

Decision-Making Through Jnana Yoga

When leaders tap into Jnana:

- They ask *"What truly matters?"* instead of *"What will look good?"*
- They balance logic and ethics, not just instinct and pressure.
- They shift from fear-based urgency to vision-based clarity.

They don't just ride the train — they navigate it mindfully.

Final Reflection: Are You Riding Consciously?

Ask yourself:

- **Am I aware of where this train is really going?**
- **Do I act from ego or from understanding?**
- **Do I question what's real and what's just noise?**

True success isn't about arriving early —
it's about getting off at the *right* station.

So... are you letting life take you wherever, or are you choosing your track with *clarity and courage*?

Nine

Sthitaprajna – The Quiet Seat in the Storm

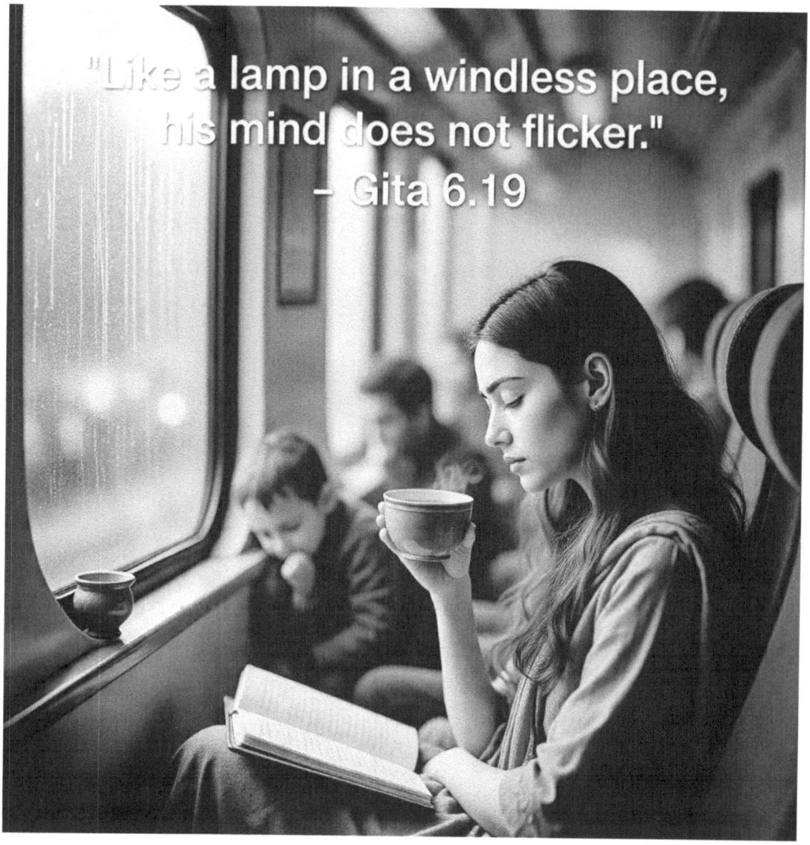

The wind outside howled. The train rattled slightly over uneven tracks. Vendors shouted. People murmured about delays. A child cried in the next compartment.

But Avantika sat still, gazing out the window, sipping warm chai – not in denial of the noise, but rooted in something deeper.

"Somewhere inside me," she wrote in her journal,
"there is a place untouched by all this motion."

She had entered the **station of Sthitaprajna** – where the **soul stays**

unmoved even when the world shakes.

The State of Sthitaprajna – Calm Amidst Chaos

Sthita = Steady

Prajna = Wisdom

In the Bhagavad Gita (2.56–2.70), Krishna describes this as the hallmark of a person of steady wisdom — one who is:

- Not elated by pleasure
- Not disturbed by pain
- Free from attachment, fear, and anger

"Like a candle flame in a windless room," Krishna says, "unwavering, bright, and serene."

Train Analogy: Sthitaprajna — Riding Through Storms with Stillness

Spiritual Quality → Life Meaning → Train Analogy

- Emotional Ups & Downs → Success/failure, praise/blame → Train delays, shaky tracks, loud stations
- Inner Stability → Peaceful detachment → Calm passenger meditating or reading quietly
- Viveka (Discernment) → Choosing what matters → Ignoring noisy vendors or useless announcements
- Detachment → Non-clinging to comfort or pain → Not obsessing over luxury or discomfort

1. Life Is a Bumpy Ride — But You Don't Have to Be

Just as trains rattle through tunnels, rush through curves, or pause at crowded stations — life throws:

- Highs (success, applause, comfort)
- Lows (loss, criticism, failure)
- Delays (unmet goals, waiting periods)

But **Sthitaprajna** is the state where:
"The soul watches it all, yet is not shaken."

2. The Wise Passenger — Calm in All Weather

Avantika looked around — some passengers panicked, some argued, some constantly checked arrival time.

But she had learned to **breathe through delays**, **smile through discomfort**, and **rest in stillness**.

"This moment too is part of the journey," she reminded herself.

Whether praised or blamed, promoted or paused — a **Sthitaprajna leader** doesn't react impulsively.

They *respond*, from centered awareness.

3. Steadiness in Leadership — Viveka Over Drama

Every five minutes, a vendor passed shouting snacks.

People around jumped up each time, distracted, craving, restless.

But Avantika had become selective — **not every voice deserved her attention.**

In leadership too:

- Don't react to every trend, fear, or opinion.
- Ask: *Does this align with Dharma? Is this worth my peace?*

This is **Viveka** — wise discernment.

4. Detachment — Knowing It's Just a Seat, Not the Self

Whether Avantika sat in an air-conditioned berth or a wooden bench, she remembered:

"I am not this seat. I am the **traveler**."

A **Sthitaprajna leader** knows:

- Wealth and title are like train seats — useful, not defining.
- Discomfort is temporary.
- Praise is passing.

And so, they stay **balanced, awake, and inwardly free**.

Leadership Reflections from Sthitaprajna

Gita Insight → Leadership Parallel

- Calm in all weather → Emotional intelligence in crises
- Not reactive to noise → Focused amidst market chaos
- Detachment from results → Integrity over popularity
- Discernment (Viveka) → Knowing what deserves attention and what doesn't

Avantika's Inner Shift

"Earlier, every small jolt made me anxious," she reflected.

"Now I realize — the train is allowed to shake. But I don't have to."

This was no longer just a spiritual journey. It was **embodied wisdom** — alive in her reactions, her pauses, her choices.

Final Reflection: Are You Riding from the Center or the Surface?

Ask yourself:

- Are you still when things go wrong?
- Do you get carried away by praise or broken by criticism?
- Or are you seated inside — aware, awake, and watching?

Be like the flame in the moving train —
Swaying on the outside, but never extinguished inside.

Ten

Dhyana Yoga – The Inner Window Seat

The train was moving swiftly now. Outside, trees blurred into a green haze. Children played near the tracks. Vendors called from platforms. Inside the coach, voices rose and fell like background music.

Avantika sat by the window, spine straight, eyes closed.

"Let me be still," she whispered.

"Let me feel the rhythm beneath the rush."

She had reached the next stop in her journey: **Dhyana Yoga — the station of inner stillness**.

Here, she wouldn't move. She would **watch the mind**, not run after it.

Train Analogy: Dhyana Yoga — Watching the Scenery Without Getting Pulled

Spiritual Insight → Leadership Parallel → Train Analogy

- Moving thoughts → Distractions, stress, information overload → The changing scenery flashing past the window
- Meditation (Dhyana) → Focused awareness, mental clarity → Sitting still and watching without reacting
- Inner silence → Creativity, intuition, peace → Hearing the hum of the train beneath the external noise
- Self-awareness (Atman) → Authenticity, grounded leadership presence → Knowing you're the passenger, not the passing scenes

1. Mind = The Scenery Outside the Window

Avantika realized:

- Her thoughts were like scenes rushing past — fast, colorful, sometimes chaotic.
- If she kept staring at them, she would forget where she was.

In leadership too:

"If you're caught in every email, every reaction, every crisis — you forget the bigger journey."

The mind *moves*. But **you** can **stay still.**

2. Meditation = Sitting Still & Watching

So, she practiced.

Every morning and evening, she sat... even when restless, even when the train rocked.

At first, thoughts pulled her like passing hawkers selling opinions:

- *"Check your phone."*
- *"You forgot that meeting."*
- *"What if this doesn't work out?"*

But slowly, her **breath became her anchor.**

And like a passenger no longer distracted by every window view — she returned to herself.

"I am not my thoughts. I am the one watching them."

3. Inner Silence = The Hidden Rhythm Beneath

After a while, she stopped hearing the noise.

Instead, she felt the train's **subtle hum** — that deep, peaceful vibration beneath all activity.

In meditation, this is the gift:

- Beneath the chaos, there's calm.
- Beneath the chatter, there's clarity.
- Beneath the self-image, there's the Self.

That's where intuitive leadership is born — not from analysis, but awareness.

4. Self-Awareness = The Passenger, Not the View

People often get lost in the journey — in roles, goals, reactions.

But Avantika remembered:

"I am not the window. I am not the noise. I am the traveler."

Dhyana Yoga taught her:

- You are not the moving mind.
- You are the unmoving witness — the **Atman**.

From that center, decisions became clearer.
Emotions no longer overwhelmed.
Purpose returned — not from striving, but from **sitting still**.

Leadership Reflection — Train the Mind, Lead from Within

1. Mind = The Scenery Outside the Window
Avantika realized:

- Her thoughts were like scenes rushing past — fast, colorful, sometimes chaotic.
- If she kept staring at them, she would forget where she was.

In leadership too:
"If you're caught in every email, every reaction, every crisis — you forget the bigger journey."
The mind *moves*. But **you** can **stay still.**

2. Meditation = Sitting Still & Watching
So, she practiced.
Every morning and evening, she sat… even when restless, even when the train rocked.
At first, thoughts pulled her like passing hawkers selling opinions:

- *"Check your phone."*
- *"You forgot that meeting."*
- *"What if this doesn't work out?"*

But slowly, her **breath became her anchor**.

And like a passenger no longer distracted by every window view — she returned to herself.

"I am not my thoughts. I am the one watching them."

3. Inner Silence = The Hidden Rhythm Beneath

After a while, she stopped hearing the noise.

Instead, she felt the train's **subtle hum** — that deep, peaceful vibration beneath all activity.

In meditation, this is the gift:

- Beneath the chaos, there's calm.
- Beneath the chatter, there's clarity.
- Beneath the self-image, there's the Self.

That's where intuitive leadership is born — not from analysis, but awareness.

4. Self-Awareness = The Passenger, Not the View

People often get lost in the journey — in roles, goals, reactions.

But Avantika remembered:

"I am not the window. I am not the noise. I am the traveler."

Dhyana Yoga taught her:

- You are not the moving mind.
- You are the unmoving witness — the **Atman**.

From that center, decisions became clearer.

Emotions no longer overwhelmed.

Purpose returned — not from striving, but from **sitting still**.

Leadership Reflection — Train the Mind, Lead from Within

Dhyana Yoga Teaching → Leadership Insight

- Observe without reaction → Emotional control in tense moments
- Still the mind → Overcome overwhelm and overthinking
- Tune into inner silence → Unlock creativity and vision
- Return to Self → Lead with authenticity and calm presence

Final Reflection: Are You Riding the Train... or Running After the Scenery?

Ask yourself:

- Do you get pulled by every distraction or stay centered?
- Are you watching your thoughts or caught in them?
- Can you sit still long enough to hear your deeper guidance?

"Dhyana Yoga is not about escaping the train," Avantika smiled,

"It's about sitting still inside it — and finding peace in the motion."

Eleven

Love the One Driving the Train – Bhakti Yoga and Surrender

* * *

The train had now entered a long stretch of quiet beauty — golden fields rolled like silk outside the window, dotted with grazing cows and distant temple spires. A gentle breeze slipped through the gap in the window, brushing Avantika's cheek like a whisper.

She felt peaceful… but something stirred within her.

Despite everything she had learned — about purpose, discipline, duty, and intellect — there was still a question in her heart:

"Am I really trusting this journey? Or am I just pretending to?"

Just then, the familiar conductor appeared again — but this time, he wasn't holding charts or clipboards.

He was simply holding a **flower garland.**

"Welcome to Station 11," he smiled gently.

"Bhakti Yoga — Love the One Driving the Train."

Are You Just Riding... or Trusting the Driver?

They walked toward the front of the train. Not into the engine room, but into a small, serene cabin with a single cushion, a bell, and a window facing forward.

"This," said the conductor, "is the Bhakti Coach."

Avantika looked around. It felt different from the others. Lighter. Warmer.

"Bhakti," he continued, "is not about knowing the train or fixing its parts.

It's about trusting the **Driver.**

It's about falling in love with the journey, because you've fallen in love with the One guiding it."

She sat quietly, absorbing his words.

The Train Analogy: Bhakti Yoga & Surrender

Concept → What It Represents → Train Analogy

- Bhakti → Loving devotion and trust in the Divine → Trusting the train system to reach your station
- Surrender → Letting go of ego control → Relaxing in your seat — trusting the driver
- Ego → Illusion of control → A passenger trying to argue with the conductor
- Divine Guidance → Krishna leading the journey → Allowing the train to flow as per Divine design

The conductor leaned toward her.

"You see, Avantika — Bhakti is when you stop clinging to the map... and start trusting the **Driver's heart**."

1. Bhakti = Trusting the Divine System

Avantika remembered moments when things hadn't gone her way. Deadlines missed. Dreams delayed. Detours that made no sense.

But looking back — they had led her to exactly where she needed to be.

"Just like you trust a train to reach the next station," the conductor said,

"Bhakti is trusting **Krishna's plan** — even when the view is foggy."

She breathed out softly, as if releasing years of silent resistance.

2. Surrender = Letting Krishna Drive

"A Bhakta doesn't demand to sit in the engine," the conductor said.

"They sit in the heart. And from there... they listen. They love. They follow the whisper of the soul."

Avantika closed her eyes.

She saw herself, once anxious and controlling — constantly checking the route, fearing delays, questioning stops.

Now... she imagined herself sitting peacefully, knowing the Driver was none other than Krishna Himself.

"My job," she whispered, "is not to control the ride.

My job is to surrender... and love the One who leads it."

3. Ego = Trying to Control the Journey

"Imagine," said the conductor, "a passenger insisting they know better.

Trying to shout directions. Panicking over every curve."

"That's ego," he smiled.

Avantika chuckled softly. She had been *that* passenger — more times than she could count.

"Bhakti," he said, "melts that ego. It replaces fear with **faith**.

Control with **compassion**.

Worry with **worship**."

She looked out the front window. The track stretched forward — unknown, infinite, beautiful.

4. Bhakti Leadership = Serving with Love

The conductor now placed the garland in her hands.

"In Bhakti," he said, "you don't lead from above.

You lead from within.

You lead with love, not logic. With surrender, not superiority."

Avantika thought of her team — the people she worked with, guided, inspired.

"Real leadership," she wrote in her journal,

"isn't about controlling people.

It's about serving a higher purpose — together."

Leadership Mirror: Bhakti in Action

Bhakti Value → Leadership Expression

- Trust in Divine Plan → Making decisions from faith, not fear
- Loving Surrender → Leading from heart and humility
- Non-Egoic Service → Empowering others without needing control
- Devotional Inspiration → Creating a purpose-driven, soulful culture

Bhagavad Gita Insight

"Among all yogis, the one with loving faith who surrenders unto Me —

is the most intimately united with Me in Yoga." — *Gita 6.47*

Avantika's Journal Entry

*"Today I understood...
My mind may plan.
My intellect may decide.
But my soul... my soul must **surrender in love**.
And when I lead from that space —
not just projects succeed...
hearts blossom."*

Final Takeaway: Who's Driving Your Train?

- Are you constantly checking the route... or enjoying the ride?
- Are you resisting detours... or surrendering with trust?
- Are you leading from the mind... or from the heart?

With Bhakti, every station is sacred.
Every delay has a reason.
Every journey becomes a **love song to the Divine**.
Love the One driving your train... and the entire ride becomes holy.

Twelve

Travel Light – Detachment & Renunciation

The train now entered a quieter stretch of land — vast meadows, empty skies, and a stillness that seemed to echo inwards.

Avantika gazed out, her reflection merging with the landscape on the windowpane.

Her journal lay open, but she hadn't written for a while.

She was thinking… but more than that, she was *carrying* — thoughts of deadlines, people's expectations, past regrets, future goals.

Her shoulders, though still, felt heavy.

Just then, a small *ding* sounded overhead.

The speaker crackled softly:

"Next Station: Detachment & Renunciation. Please check your luggage."

Avantika blinked. *"Luggage?"*

The conductor appeared once more, this time holding a **scales chart** and a faded cloth bag.

"Welcome," he said, "to **Station 12: Travel Light.**"

Did You Bring Too Much Luggage?

He motioned toward a scale in the corner of the coach.

Avantika placed her bag on it.

But instead of clothes or books, it displayed… emotions.

Regret. Fear. Control. Expectation. Pride. Guilt.

"Many travelers," he whispered, "suffer not because the ride is hard — but because they packed too much inside."

The Train Analogy: Detachment & Letting Go

Concept → What It Represents → Train Analogy

- Attachments → Clinging to outcomes, roles, possessions → A traveler dragging heavy luggage through the aisle
- Detachment (Vairagya) → Letting go while still engaging → Traveling light — present, but unburdened
- Renunciation (Tyaga) → Acting without ego or ownership → Doing your duty, but knowing it's not your train
- Control Anxiety → Worrying over what's not in your hands → Constantly checking bags, fearing loss
- Freedom → Ease, clarity, peace → Moving freely, resting deeply, serving joyfully

1. Attachment = Heavy Baggage

Avantika imagined a traveler pulling three massive suitcases through the aisle, bumping into everyone, sweating, exhausted.

"That's us," the conductor said,

"When we carry every memory, every expectation, every 'should-have-been' on our back."

"I didn't realize how much I was holding," Avantika thought.

"Not just tasks — but identities. Titles. Applause. Control."

2. Detachment = Traveling Light

The conductor handed her the faded cloth bag.

It was light — but had everything essential.

"Detachment," he said, "is not indifference.

It's participation *without possession.*"

Avantika nodded slowly.

"You can still love deeply," he added, "but without clinging.

Still act fully — but without *needing* a result."

She felt something soften in her chest.

Freedom, she realized, comes from knowing you're not your baggage.

3. Renunciation = Doing Without Owning

"Imagine helping a fellow traveler," said the conductor, "and then declaring, 'I fixed your journey!'"

Avantika smiled — she'd done that.

"True renunciation," he continued,

"is doing your part with full sincerity…

but not *owning* the outcomes."

She saw it clearly now.

It's not about quitting work. It's about quitting ego.

You clean your seat. You serve chai. You guide another passenger.

But you don't claim ownership of the train.

"Do your karma — but don't carry the credit," she scribbled in her journal.

4. Inner Freedom = Less Control, More Trust

"Why do we suffer?" the conductor asked.

"Because we want the train to stop where *we* want.

Because we want no delays, no detours, no discomfort."

"But peace," he smiled, "comes when you trust the Driver.

And travel only with what's essential."

Avantika breathed in.

She imagined handing over her bags — her need for perfection, for praise, for guarantees — to Krishna.

And suddenly, the ride felt… lighter.

Leadership Mirror: What Are You Holding On To?

Spiritual Value → Leadership Expression

- Vairagya (Detachment) → Leading without emotional volatility or fear
- Tyaga (Renunciation) → Delegating, empowering, working without ego
- Control → Trust Shift → Allowing space for team autonomy and divine flow
- Freedom from Outcome → Innovating fearlessly, staying balanced in results

Avantika's Journal Entry

"Today I learned that I can still show up fully...

Without tying myself to outcomes.

That I can serve...

Without needing recognition.

That I can love...

Without fearing loss."
"And maybe," she smiled,
"that's what it means to travel light — to lead with grace, not grip."

Final Takeaway: What's in Your Bag?

- Are you carrying outdated stories, expectations, and regrets?
- Are you leading with presence, or pressure?
- Can you act without ownership? Love without clinging? Lead without controlling?

True travelers move lightly.
True leaders lead freely.
And those who surrender their luggage at this station…
ride the rest of the way with peace in their hearts and wings on their soul.

Thirteen

Train Delays & Troubles – Resilience & Patience

The clouds had thickened outside.

Thunder rumbled faintly in the distance as the train began to slow… then stopped.

Avantika looked around. Passengers exchanged puzzled glances. A murmur spread: "Is there a problem on the track?"

She checked the time — they were behind schedule.

She sighed and shut her journal.

Her thoughts began to swirl: *"Why now? What if I miss something important? What if this messes up everything?"*

Just then, the familiar voice rang over the speaker:

"Dear passengers, we are experiencing a delay. Please stay calm. This, too, is part of the journey."

And right on cue, the conductor appeared — this time in a thick raincoat, his lantern glowing dimly through the mist.

"Welcome," he said gently, "to **Station 13: Resilience & Patience.**"

Is Your Train Late? Can You Stay Peaceful?

He motioned toward a bench beside the window.

"This," he said, "is where many travelers lose heart.

Delays, detours, and discomforts — they test your patience.

But they're not the end. They're just… pauses."

Avantika leaned back. *"So what do I do?"*

The conductor smiled.

"You practice **Titiksha** — the strength to endure, and the grace to wait."

The Train Analogy: Building Resilience & Patience

The clouds had thickened outside.

Thunder rumbled faintly in the distance as the train began to slow… then stopped.

Avantika looked around. Passengers exchanged puzzled glances. A murmur spread: "Is there a problem on the track?"

She checked the time — they were behind schedule.

She sighed and shut her journal.

Her thoughts began to swirl: *"Why now? What if I miss something important? What if this messes up everything?"*

Just then, the familiar voice rang over the speaker:

"Dear passengers, we are experiencing a delay. Please stay calm. This, too, is part of the journey."

And right on cue, the conductor appeared — this time in a thick raincoat, his lantern glowing dimly through the mist.

"Welcome," he said gently, "to **Station 13: Resilience & Patience.**"

Is Your Train Late? Can You Stay Peaceful?

He motioned toward a bench beside the window.

"This," he said, "is where many travelers lose heart.

Delays, detours, and discomforts — they test your patience.

But they're not the end. They're just... pauses."

Avantika leaned back. *"So what do I do?"*

The conductor smiled.

"You practice **Titiksha** — the strength to endure, and the grace to wait."

The Train Analogy: Building Resilience & Patience

Concept → What It Represents → Train Analogy

- Challenges & Obstacles → Setbacks, struggles, failures → A train facing rough weather or signal delays
- Resilience (Titiksha) → Steadiness through difficulty → The train continues, no matter the weather
- Patience (Dhairya) → Calm endurance, without agitation → A traveler waiting peacefully at a station
- Trust & Faith → Confidence in the journey's unfolding → Believing the system will get you to your station

1. Challenges = Delays, Storms & Signal Stops

Avantika looked outside — trees swayed, and rain tapped the glass.

"Life," the conductor said, "will often pause you when you least expect it.

Not to punish… but to prepare."

💭 She recalled her own moments of breakdown — job loss, rejection letters, creative blocks.

"At first, they felt like the end," she whispered. "But later… I realized they were reshaping me."

The conductor nodded, "Storms don't stop the train — they just make you slow down. Listen deeper. Breathe better."

2. Resilience = The Train Keeps Moving

He led her to the engine room.

Despite the weather, the wheels were still turning — slower, but steady.

"This," he said, "is **Titiksha** — resilience. The power to keep going, even when the road is tough."

Avantika reflected:

- She'd felt defeated before — but she always got up.
- She'd faced fear — and still walked forward.
- She'd cried — but she'd never quit.

"True strength isn't loud," she wrote, *"It's silent persistence."*

3. Patience = Waiting Calmly at the Station

They walked past a waiting area.

A mother was humming to her child. An old man sipped chai. A student read his book — calm, accepting, serene.

"This," the conductor whispered, "is **Dhairya** — patience.

It's not passive. It's powerful."

"Sometimes," he continued, "you must wait for life to realign. For the next door to open. For your inner readiness to catch up."

Avantika closed her eyes.

Maybe this delay isn't stopping me, she thought. *Maybe it's saving me.*

4. Faith = Trusting the System

Back in her seat, the lights flickered... then glowed steadily again.

"We don't see the whole map," said the conductor, "but we can trust the One who does."

He pointed to a tiny sticker on the window:

"Trust the Train. Respect the Delay. Stay steady in storms."

"Patience isn't waiting for time to pass," Avantika scribbled,

"It's how you behave while time is passing."

Leadership Mirror: Strength in Setbacks

Spiritual Value → Leadership Reflection

- Titiksha (Resilience) → Leading through storms without emotional collapse
- Dhairya (Patience) → Choosing long-term wisdom over quick fixes
- Trust in Divine Timing → Allowing ideas to ripen; not forcing outcomes
- Growth through Setbacks → Turning failures into learning and quiet strength

Avantika's Journal Entry

"Today I was reminded:

- *Delays don't mean denial.*
- *Setbacks are sacred too.*
- *And the strongest leaders are those who keep moving — even when it rains."*

"My job is not to control the speed...
But to stay grounded in storms and trust the direction."

Final Takeaway: Are You Strong in the Storm?

- Are you reacting to every challenge, or responding with resilience?
- Are you rushing the journey, or trusting divine timing?
- The train will move again. Will you be ready when it does?

Strength isn't just in speeding ahead — it's in staying calm when nothing moves.

And that... is the quiet power of Titiksha.

Fourteen

Train Announcer & Guide – The Power of the Guru

The train picked up speed again after the delay. The sky had cleared, but a light fog still hugged the edges of the fields.

Avantika leaned back, feeling the calm after the storm of stillness.

Suddenly, the speakers crackled.

"Next station... approaching in five minutes. Please prepare to disembark if this is your stop."

The message was clear. Helpful. Timely.

She smiled.

"How do they always know exactly when and what to say?" she wondered aloud.

As if on cue, the conductor appeared — this time not with tools or charts, but with a **whistle, a timetable, and a small ancient book** tucked under his arm.

"Welcome," he said gently, "to **Station 14: Guru — The Train Announcer & Guide.**"

Can You Hear the Voice Guiding You?

Avantika sat up.

The conductor looked out the window. "Most people are on the right train... but still don't know where they're going. Or when to get off. Or what the signs mean."

"That's why we need a **Guru,**" he said, "someone who's walked the track before. Someone who knows the stops — and what each one asks of you."

Guru (Mentorship & Spiritual Guidance)

- Seek wisdom from someone who *lives* what they teach
- Mentors turn maps into movement

The Train Analogy: The Role of a Guru

Concept → What It Represents → Train Analogy

- Guru (Spiritual Guide) → Enlightened teacher on the spiritual path → The conductor who ensures the train stays on track
- Disciple (Seeker) → One who learns and grows → A trusting passenger following the announcements
- Sacred Teachings → Divine knowledge and direction → Timetables,

maps, and signal systems
- Doubts & Confusion → Inner uncertainty or ego resistance → Taking wrong trains or getting off too early
- Faith & Surrender → Trusting the process with humility → Believing the driver knows the way, even if you don't

1. Guru = The Conductor (Knows the Route)

Avantika imagined herself traveling in a foreign land — unfamiliar stops, strange names.

"Without the conductor," he said, "you might disembark at the wrong place… or never reach your destination."

In her own life:

- She had followed influencers who talked but didn't *live* wisdom.
- She'd doubted her own inner guidance.
- But her real growth began only when she surrendered to a teacher who *walked their talk.*

"A Guru doesn't just inform," she wrote, *"They transform."*

2. The Seeker = The Passenger (Must Listen & Trust)

The conductor leaned in:

"Some passengers don't listen. They jump out mid-way, thinking they know better… and get lost."

"Others ignore the signs — then wonder why they missed their station."

Avantika nodded slowly. *"I've done both."*

"A wise seeker," he continued, "stays alert, listens deeply, and *trusts* the conductor — especially when the path seems unclear."

3. Sacred Teachings = The Railway Map

He handed her the tiny book.

It was marked with symbols and verses from the Gita, Upanishads, and ancient wisdom.

"This," he said, "is the **map.**

But without someone who understands it... you may read it wrong."

Avantika recalled how, before meeting her teacher, the Gita had felt too abstract.

But once it was *explained with love and depth,* every verse became alive.

"The map isn't enough — you need a guide who speaks its language," she whispered.

4. Doubts = Wrong Trains & Misguided Stops

He showed her a list:

"Popular Destinations That Aren't the Goal"

- Fame Junction
- Approval Station
- Comfortville
- Shortcut Loop

"So many stop here," he said, "thinking they've arrived.

But they miss the true destination: Self-realization."

Avantika sighed. *"I've chased some of these, too."*

"Doubt makes you switch trains," he said. "Faith keeps you moving."

5. Faith = Letting the Conductor Lead

Finally, he pointed to the horizon — the next station glowed in the morning sun.

"Not every path is visible. But the Guru knows the light behind the fog."

"Even when I don't know the track ahead," Avantika wrote, *"I can trust*

the one holding the lantern."

Leadership Mirror: Wisdom Needs a Guide

Spiritual Insight → Leadership Expression

- Guru Tattva → Having mentors, coaches, and wise advisors
- Trust in Guidance → Leaning on senior wisdom, especially during crisis
- Scriptures as Maps → Clarity from core values, vision, and principles
- Confusion Without Guru → Chaos from lack of clarity or ego-driven leadership
- Surrender & Coachability → Staying humble, learning constantly

Avantika's Journal Entry

"Today I learned...

- *I don't have to know it all. I just have to trust the one who does.*
- *My map is not enough without a guide who knows the terrain.*
- *Mentorship isn't weakness — it's the secret doorway to strength."*

Final Takeaway: Who's Guiding Your Journey?

- Are you listening to the right voices, or the loudest ones?
- Do you have a guide who knows the destination — and how to get there?
- Every great traveler has a wise conductor.

The journey is long. Don't go alone. The right Guru doesn't just show you the next stop — they reveal the path home.

Fifteen

Moksha Junction – Surrender to Krishna

The sun had begun to set.

The sky outside the window painted shades of lavender and gold, as if bowing gently to the closing of a long journey. Avantika sat quietly, her journal closed, her pen resting. This time… there were no questions in her mind.

Only a silence. Deep. Expansive.

The conductor appeared — not with papers or instructions — but with **folded hands and a radiant smile**.

"Welcome," he whispered, "to **Moksha Junction — Final Destination.**"

Are You Ready to Disembark?

He didn't rush. He didn't explain.

He simply looked at her with knowing eyes.

"When you surrender fully," he said, "you don't have to plan the rest of the journey. You just trust... that Krishna will take you home."

Surrender to Krishna → The Ultimate Realization

- All paths lead back to the Divine
- Peace is not found in control — but in complete trust
- Surrender is not weakness — it is the highest intelligence

The Train Analogy: Letting Krishna Take the Controls

Concept → What It Represents → Train Analogy

- Krishna (Supreme Guide) → Divine intelligence and protection → The Train Tracks & System guiding all journeys
- Surrender (Śaraṇāgati) → Letting go of ego and control → Relaxing in your seat, trusting the train's course
- Doubts & Worries → Fear and mental resistance → Asking the driver to stop at every signal
- Material Attachments → Clinging to ego, identity, expectations → Carrying too much luggage — tiring and unnecessary
- Bhakti (Devotion) → Loving trust in the Divine → A first-class seat — peaceful, joyful, anchored

1. Krishna = The Train System (Guiding the Journey)

The conductor pointed gently out the window.

"You don't see the whole track... but that doesn't mean the track isn't there."

"Krishna's path is like this railway system — even if you don't know the next station, He does. He always has."

In Avantika's life:

- She tried to plan every detail.
- She feared wrong turns and delays.
- But now... she could finally let go.

Because **He** was in charge.

2. Surrender – Relaxing Into the Journey

The coach was still. The other passengers, too, seemed quieter — reflective.

The conductor placed his hand gently on the seat beside her.

"Surrender," he said, "is knowing that you were *never* the driver. You were always the *beloved traveler.*"

"Let go. Let Him lead. Just love — and be led."

3. Doubts = Questioning Every Stop

Avantika smiled to herself, remembering earlier moments:

- Panicking over her career
- Worrying about what others thought
- Trying to control outcomes and timelines

"I asked the conductor a thousand times, 'Are we going the right way?'" she laughed.

Now she knew better.

"Every station I doubted... was part of the plan all along."

4. Material Attachments = Carrying Heavy Baggage

He pointed to a woman dragging a suitcase down the aisle — puffing, grumbling, exhausted.

"That," he said, "is what ego does. It weighs us down with control, expectation, fear, and regret."

"You don't need all that. Just bring your love."

Avantika had carried burdens for years. But Bhakti taught her to **unpack.**

Now she traveled light — and free.

5. Bhakti = A First-Class Ticket Home

She remembered Gita 18.66:

"Abandon all other dharmas. Surrender to Me. I shall deliver you. Do not fear."

This wasn't about giving up.

It was about giving **in** — to love, to grace, to Him.

"Bhakti is the heart's seatbelt — you still ride the train, but you ride safely... in Krishna's care."

Avantika's Final Journal Entry

"Today, I didn't write to figure anything out.
I just wrote to say thank you.
For the delays.
For the lessons.
For the love I didn't always recognize.
And above all — thank you, Krishna...
for driving the train when I didn't know how."

Final Takeaway: Are You Still Trying to Steer?

- Are you trying to control life's route — or resting in trust?
- Are you clinging to outcomes — or traveling light with grace?
- Are you riding with devotion — knowing Krishna has your destination in hand?

Moksha isn't a place. It's a moment.

The moment you finally let go… and fall into the arms of the Divine Conductor.

Leadership Parallel: From Control to Divine Service

Spiritual Realization → Leadership Expression

- Surrender → Leading without ego — guided by purpose, not pride
- Bhakti-Driven Action → Serving with love, not control
- Letting Go of Outcomes → Long-term vision over short-term anxiety
- Divine Trust → Anchoring decisions in clarity, grace, and faith
- Final Liberation (Moksha) → Leaving a legacy of service, not self

Final Reflection

Avantika looked out one last time — fields turning golden under the twilight.

She smiled.

The train didn't need her to steer.

She just had to **be present, be grateful… and trust.**

Because Krishna was driving.

And **every station was sacred** — even the one called *home.*

Sixteen

Hidden Compartment – The Six Inner Impurities (Sad-Ripu)

The train had almost reached the end of its line.

Avantika sat near the window, her heart light, her mind at peace. Or so she thought.

The ride had been long. Enlightening. Beautiful.

But just as she reached for her bag, ready to step off at Moksha Junction… she felt something beneath her seat.

"Is there still something left?" she wondered.

The conductor returned one last time — not with a smile, but with gentle seriousness.

"You've journeyed far," he said. "But even the most awakened passenger may be carrying hidden weight."

He knelt down, reached under the seat, and pulled out six dusty, invisible bags — small, yet strangely heavy.

"*Ṣaḍ-Ripu,* child. The six inner enemies. Before you disembark... these must be left behind."

Ṣaḍ-Ripu – The Hidden Baggage of the Soul

Inner Purification → The Key to Lasting Transformation

- Even the best passenger may still carry burdens unseen
- The journey ends not with knowledge — but with cleansing

Avantika looked at the six invisible bags.

Each carried a name, and each had once disguised itself as something noble.

Impurity → Shadow in Life → Train Analogy

- Kāma (Desire) → Craving for pleasure, control, fame → Overloading with luxuries — slowing the journey
- Krodha (Anger) → Outbursts, frustration, reactivity → Causing chaos when the train is delayed
- Lobha (Greed) → Insatiable hunger for more → Hoarding seats, food, power
- Moha (Attachment) → Clinging to roles, identities → Believing the train is your home — refusing to get off
- Mada (Pride) → Ego, superiority, resistance to feedback → Demanding special treatment, acting like you own the train

- Mātsarya (Envy) → Resentment, comparison, jealousy → Hating others for getting better seats

How This Shows Up in the Journey

1. **Impurities = Secret Weight**

- They don't shout. They whisper.
- Sometimes, they wear the mask of ambition, confidence, or "standards."

Avantika recalled moments when she had:

- Wanted recognition (Kāma)
- Snapped at delay (Krodha)
- Compared her chapter with someone else's success (Mātsarya)

Each moment was *a bag she had unknowingly packed.*

2. **Recognition = First Step to Liberation**

The conductor offered her a small mirror.
"Don't fear what you see," he said. "See it... and then let it go."
Avantika gazed into her inner landscape:

- Her unmet longings
- Her proud victories
- Her quiet comparisons

And slowly, softly... she smiled.
"I don't need these anymore."

3. **Dropping the Bags = Lighter Journey**

One by one, she placed each invisible bag on the platform.

- Kāma → at the Station of Simplicity
- Krodha → at Patience Halt
- Lobha → at the Cabin of Generosity
- Moha → at Clarity Curve
- Mada → at the Bench of Humility
- Mātsarya → at the Garden of Inspiration

She turned to the conductor.

"Now am I ready?"

He didn't answer with words.

He simply bowed.

True Leadership = Inner Cleansing

"Even if the train looks perfect outside... termites inside the wooden frame can collapse everything."

Avantika understood.

Great leaders do not just lead teams — they **conquer themselves** first.

Sad-Ripu → Shadow Expression in Leadership → Transformed Expression

- Kāma (Desire) → Overwork, ego-driven hustle → Purposeful, balanced drive
- Krodha (Anger) → Harsh decisions, reactive tone → Calm, composed leadership
- Lobha (Greed) → Hoarding, unethical shortcuts → Generous, transparent ethics
- Moha (Attachment) → Rigidity, fear of change → Adaptability, clarity
- Mada (Pride) → Power struggles, resistance → Humility, openness

- Mātsarya (Envy) → Competition, resentment → Collaboration, inspiration

Final Takeaway: What's Under Your Seat?

- Are you holding silent baggage that weighs your leadership down?
- Do you have the courage to name the invisible forces within?
- Can you let go of even the hidden weights… and rise?

The journey is not just about knowing the Gita — it is about *living it, cleaning the self,* and *walking lightly into the light.*

"The ride is sacred. The tracks are divine. But your heart must be empty of ego... to arrive fully at peace."

Moksha Isn't the End. It's the Beginning.

Avantika stepped off the train — not with baggage, but with blessings.

Her journey wasn't over. It had just begun.

Because now… **she was no longer a passenger.**

She was a **conductor** in her own right — carrying forward the wisdom, the lightness, the leadership of love.

Seventeen

Epilogue: Avantika's Final Realization – The Journey Within

The station was quiet.

The breeze was still.

Avantika stood at the edge of the platform — the train behind her, the open world ahead. But something had changed.

She no longer felt like the same woman who had boarded that train with questions swirling in her mind and a suitcase full of dreams.

She had seen every compartment of the self.

She had travelled through dharma and doubt, clarity and confusion, action and stillness. She had met her ego, her strengths, her fears — and finally, her soul.

She had arrived.

Not just at a place.

But at a **realization**:

"The journey was never out there. The stations were always within me. Each stop revealed a hidden part... until all parts became whole."

She gently sat on a bench, eyes reflecting stillness, heart beating softly with surrender.

And then, like a breeze whispering through memory, each **station** passed through her mind — one by one, not as concepts, but as companions.

The 16 Stations of Inner Leadership

1. **Dharma & Purpose** – I am here for a reason.
2. **Swadharma** – My path is sacred, even if it looks different from others.
3. **Varna System** – My role is part of the divine design.
4. **Ashrama Dharma** – Each stage of life is a sacred chapter.
5. **Three Gunas** – I am not my moods. I am the watcher.
6. **Mind & Senses Mastery** – I lead the mind, not follow it.
7. **Karma Yoga** – Do the work. Let go of the outcome.
8. **Jnana Yoga** – Discipline of wisdom is the compass I trust.
9. **Sthitaprajna** – Even in chaos, I can remain calm.
10. **Dhyana Yoga** – Silence is strength. Meditation is power.
11. **Bhakti Yoga** – Surrender makes the ride sacred.
12. **Detachment & Renunciation** – Travel light — joy doesn't need baggage.
13. **Resilience & Patience** – Delays aren't denials. Wait with faith.
14. **Guru & Mentorship** – Listen to the voice that knows the way.
15. **Surrender to Krishna** – He is the Conductor. I am the flute.
16. **The Six Inner Impurities (Sad-Ripu)** – The final battle is within. The final freedom is purity.

And then... silence.

Not empty, but *complete.*

Avantika smiled. Not because everything was perfect.

But because everything now had meaning.

"I don't need to chase anymore.

I simply need to walk — in alignment, in surrender, in love."

She rose, leaving behind her last seat on the train — lighter, clearer, fuller.

She had become what the journey had prepared her for all along:

A leader who leads not from the mind... but from the soul.

Final Reflection: What Train Are *You* On?

This isn't just Avantika's story.

It's yours too.

You, dear reader, are on your own train.

With your own stations.

Your own luggage.

Your own ticket of destiny.

And perhaps, just perhaps — this book is your conductor's voice, whispering softly:

"Watch. Reflect. Release.

And remember — you were never alone on this ride."

May your journey be sacred.

May your leadership be soulful.

And may you always know when to get off... and when to surrender.

Hari Om Tat Sat.

Eighteen

Glossary

Ashrama Vyavastha – The four stages of life in Hindu philosophy: Brahmacharya (student life), Grhastha (householder), Vanaprastha (retired/seeker), and Sannyasa (renunciation).

Bhakti Yoga – The path of devotion and surrender to the Divine, guided by love and faith.

Brahmacharya – The first stage of life in the *Āshrama Vyavastha*; a disciplined student life focused on learning and self-control.

Detachment (Vairagya) – The ability to act without clinging to outcomes or possessions, staying free from bondage.

Dhyana Yoga – The path of meditation, cultivating focus, stillness, and inner strength.

Grhastha – The second stage of life; the householder stage, where one fulfills duties of family, career, and society.

Guru – A spiritual teacher or guide who dispels ignorance and shows the path of truth.

Indriyas (Senses) – The five senses (sight, hearing, smell, taste, touch) and mind as instruments of experience; mastering them leads to inner control.

Jnana Yoga – The path of wisdom and knowledge, emphasizing discernment and self-realization.

Karma Yoga – The path of selfless action, performing duties without attachment to results.

Krishna – The Divine guide in the Bhagavad Gita, representing supreme wisdom, love, and leadership.

Manas (Mind) – The thinking, feeling, and desiring faculty; when disciplined, it becomes a servant of the Self.

Moksha – Liberation or final freedom from the cycle of birth and death; the ultimate goal of life.

Moha (Delusion/Attachment) – Clinging to illusions, relationships, or identities, leading to confusion and suffering.

Purusartha (Goals of Life) – The four aims of human life: *Dharma* (duty/righteousness), *Artha* (prosperity), *Kāma* (pleasure), and *Moksha* (liberation).

Rajas – One of the three *gunas*; the quality of passion, restlessness, and desire-driven activity.

Resilience (Titiksa) – The strength to endure difficulties with patience, faith, and equanimity.

Sannyasa – The fourth stage of life; renunciation, where one detaches from worldly concerns and focuses fully on the Divine.

Sattva – One of the three *gunas*; the quality of purity, harmony, knowledge, and light.

Saranagati (Surrender) – Complete surrender to the Divine will, letting go of ego and control.

Sthitaprajna – A person of steady wisdom who remains calm in joy and sorrow, success and failure.

Swadharma – One's own duty or path, aligned with inner nature and divine order.

Tamas – One of the three *gunas*; the quality of ignorance, inertia, and darkness.

Vairagya – See *Detachment*.

Varna System – The division of society based on inherent qualities and duties: *Brahmana* (teachers/priests), *Ksatriya* (warriors/leaders), *Vaisya* (merchants/farmers), and *Sudra* (workers/helpers).

Vanaprastha – The third stage of life; the retired stage where one gradually withdraws from material duties and turns inward.

About the Author

About the Author

Vijayshree Ratanparkhe's spiritual journey began in childhood, nurtured by a deep sense of connection with the divine. This innate spirituality led her to explore the teachings of the **Bhagavad Gita**, which resonated deeply with her soul.

Her soul's evolution, guided by the Gita, shaped her life purpose: sharing its practical wisdom to make it accessible and applicable to everyday life. Inspired by the Gita's message, she embodies **Karma Yoga**, selflessly serving others while cultivating inner wisdom.

Vijayshree's personal journey—from seeking external love to discovering true love within—has been transformative. She now shares her experiences to inspire spiritual growth in others. The **18th chapter of the Bhagavad Gita** revealed her purpose, urging her to share these timeless teachings with the world.

Her message is one of hope and inspiration, encouraging everyone to explore the Bhagavad Gita and apply its wisdom in daily life. She envisions a world where all live in harmony, guided by love, compassion, and selfless service.

Some of her favorite Bhagavad Gita verses include:

"Do your duty without attachment to its fruits." (Chapter 2, Verse 47)

"The one who has control over the mind is tranquil in heat and cold, in pleasure and pain, and in honor and disgrace." (Chapter 2, Verse 56)

"The one who sees Me everywhere and sees everything in Me, is never lost to Me, nor am I ever lost to him." (Chapter 6, Verse 30)

These verses continue to inspire her to guide others on their spiritual journeys.

You can connect with me on:

- https://shreesessencia.com
- https://x.com/Vijayshreerp
- https://www.facebook.com/shreesessencia
- https://www.linkedin.com/in/vijayshree-r-48024aa6

9 789334 405927
Printed at Repro India Ltd.